EUGENE ORE WALKS

by

Tyler Burgess

Tyler Burgess

Walk With Me
Eugene, Oregon

Published by Walk With Me
1430 Willamette St. #579
Eugene, OR 97401
541-684-4951
www.walk-with-me.com
tylerburgess@walk-with-me.com

Printed in USA

Be safe. Look both ways before crossing the
street. Be prepared for the weather. Carry
water and food on long walks. Be able to do
the distance or elevation gain.

I have walked all these routes,
but as we all know, shift happens.
Sidewalks and trails change due
to construction. Corrections
are welcome.

Mileage is measured by g-map.pedometer.com.
Base map is ODOT.

ISBN 978-0-9816599-0-9

How to Use This Book

<u>Choose a walk.</u> The summary chart lists:

- <u>Start/finish point.</u> For more options, some maps have more than one start point.

- <u>Route names</u> are listed alphabetically in the table of contents.

- <u>Miles.</u> Several maps have options for a short, flat or a longer, hilly route.

- <u>Rating.</u> E = easy, mostly flat. M = moderate, hillier with distance. H = hard, hilly and longer.

- <u>Elevation gain.</u> Number of feet going up.

- <u>Bus.</u> Public transportation to, or near, the start/finish point. Schedules change. Call LTD at 541-687-5555 or www.ltd.org.

<u>Restrooms.</u> Open year around at
        Alton Baker Park
        Amazon Parkway and 24th lot.
   Open seasonally (April to October)
        Monroe and 10th, Monroe Park
        Hilyard and 38th, Tugman Park

<u>Go.</u> Have fun exploring the trails, bike paths and neighborhoods of Eugene, Oregon.

Summary Chart of Walking Routes

Start/Finish	Route Name	Miles	Rating	Elev Gain	Bus
Agate St. & 13th	Big Trees on Campus	1.5 to 3	E	flat	Breeze, Emx
Alton Baker Park	Butte to Bakery	2.5 or 3.5	M	400	Breeze,13,79
Alton Baker Park	Historic Homes	2 to 4.7	E	flat	Breeze,13,79
Alton Baker Park	Pre's Rock	2.5 to 6.5	E/M	300	Breeze,13,79
Alton Baker Park	Spyglass	1.2 to 6.2	E	92	Breeze,13,79
Alton Baker Park	Gillespie Butte	6	M	114	Breeze,13,79
Amazon Way & 24th	Beautiful Alley	1.7 or 3	M	110	82, 92, 73
Amazon Way & 24th	Edgewood Trails I	6.4	M	498	82, 92, 73
Amazon Way & 24th	Emerald Hill	1.5 or 2.5	M	116	82, 92, 73
Amazon Way & 24th	Four Creeks	2 to 7	M/H	270/540	82, 92, 73
Amazon Way & 24th	Mansions & Meadow	4.4 to 9	M/H	834	82, 92, 73
Amazon Way & 24th	City Views	2, 3.6, 9.8	M/H	84/625	82, 92, 73
Ayres Rd. & Meadowview	Ashley Estates	1 or 2	E	flat	none
Brae Burn Dr. & 40th	Edgewood Exploring	1	M	108	none
Buck St. & 15th	Hawkins Haunts	2 to 5.3	E/M	30/347	30, 32, 37, 78
Charnelton St. & 17th	Cornucopia	1 to 3.1	E	50	36, 78
Clinton & Debrick	Gillespie Butte	1	M	104	60
Delta Hwy & Green Acres	Pretty Ponds	3	E	flat	66, 67
Donald St. & 40th	Edgewood Trails II	2.4	M	222	73
Fox Hollow & Christensen	Ridgeline to Summit	3.4	H	1,105	none
Gilham & Honeywood	Honeywood Hop	2 to 4.2	E	flat	66, 67
Gilham & Lakeview Dr.	Christmas Lights	1.5	E	flat	none
Hilyard & 38th	Ridgeline Long Loop	10.3	H	hilly	25, 28
Jefferson St. & 15th	Friendly St. Loop	3.5 to 5.5	E/M	flat/434	33, 36, 78
Jefferson, Rose Garden	Rose Garden Route	4, 6	E	flat	51
Lane Community College	Labrynith & Trails	.5 to 3	E/M	130	81,82,85,98
Martin Dr. & Canyon Dr.	Ridgeline Short loop	0.5	M	101	25, 28
Monroe & 10th	Sweet Life Loop	1.5 to 4	E	flat	51
Monroe & 27th	City Views	7.7	H	599	33
Several access points	Ridgeline Trail Map	6.3	E/M/H	hilly	25, 28
Several access points	Fern Ridge Bike Path	up to 14	E	flat	41, 43
Several access points	River Bike Path	up to 14	E	flat	Breeze,13,79
University St. & 24th	Elk Street	1.5 to 3.1	E	135	27
University St. & 24th	Fairmount Trail	2, 2.5, 4	M	flat/227	27
Valley River Mall	Pretty Ponds	3 to 8.7	E	flat	Bree,60,66,67
Valley River Mall	Gillespie Butte	3	M	114	Bree,60,66,67
Willamette & 52nd	Ridgeline to Summit	4.4	H	1,109	none
Willamette, SB Park	Ridgeline to Summit	1	H	791	none

4 **Rating: E = Easy, M = Moderate, H = Hard**

MAP to START POINTS

Map not to exact scale.

Contents

Legend

.... shorter route

⚞ hill

T = toilet **P** = parking

food = grocery, market, or cafe. Do buy
    something if you use facilities.

mi. = mileage

R = right. **L** = left.

elevation = feet of ascent

7

Introduction

These walking routes are mostly an accumulation of walks I have led as a marathon walking instructor.

 Many thanks to the hundreds of people who walked with me. You made all walks more fun and interesting.

Walking Tips

1. Take a smaller, or shorter, step. Short, quick steps lessen impact on joints and increase speed.

2. Walk by minutes, not miles. Start with 10 to 20 minute walks. Add 5 minutes to daily walks every two weeks. Goal: walk one hour a day for the rest of your life.

3. Start each walk slowly. Build to a brisk pace, with ability to talk. Walk slowly to cool down at the end of each walk.

4. Wear good walking, running shoes or boots. Get good gear and go outside every day.

5. Stretch afterwards. Walking tightens the muscles on the back of your legs, pulling the joints together. It does not hurt, at first!

  ⓐ hold this stretch one minute on each side.

  ⓑ Stretch up, then down 5 times.

ASHLEY ESTATES

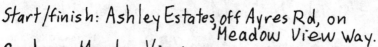

Distance: 1 mi. or 2 mi. Flat.

Start/finish: Ashley Estates, off Ayres Rd, on Meadow View Way.

Go down Meadow View.
Right at end, onto Mirror Pond Way.
(for 1 mi. option,
R on Quail Meadow.)
follow map at ＊.

R on Gilham.
R on Don Juan.
R at corner, Sterling Woods.
L on Crimson Ave.
         L on Quail Meadows.
＊ **R** at next corner, River Pointe Dr.
         R on Ayres, back to finish.

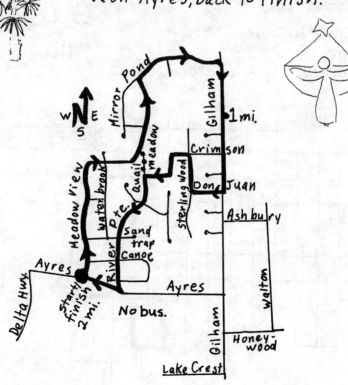

BEAUTIFUL ALLEY

Distance: 1.7 mi., 3 mi. Elevation gain: 110 ft.

Start/finish: 24th and Amazon parking lot.

R from parking lot, on 24th.
L on Portland. R on 25th.
R on Olive. R on 24th one block.
L on McMillan to end. L up hill.
L on Olive.   (Grandview.)

19th and Olive. Columbia College 1856-1860 Basalt marker.
site of Columbia College

(for 1.7mi. R on Olive. R on 19th.)
(see * below.

R on 23rd. R on Monroe.
L on 21st for half a block.
R in to alley.
R at end of alley, 20th street.

2210 Olive
English Cottage Style

L on Washington.
R on 19th   *
R on bike path before school.

view of Coburg Hills on Grandview Street

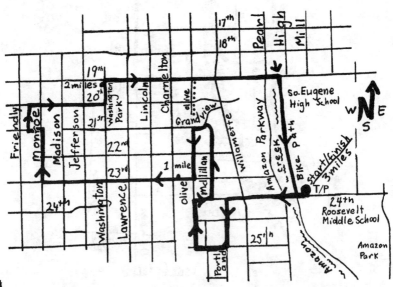

10

CHRISTMAS LIGHTS

Distance: 1.5 mi. Flat, on sidewalks.

Start/finish: 2100 Lakeview, corner of Gilham and Lakeview Dr.
R, or south, at Northridge (house 3153)
L on Elkhorn.
R on Lakeview.
R on Marie Ln.
R on Sarah Ln.

L on Crescent Dr.
L on Cheryl
L into Pine Grove culdesac, then Straight on Pine Grove

L on Parkview Dr., 1 block.
L on Lakeview, back to start.

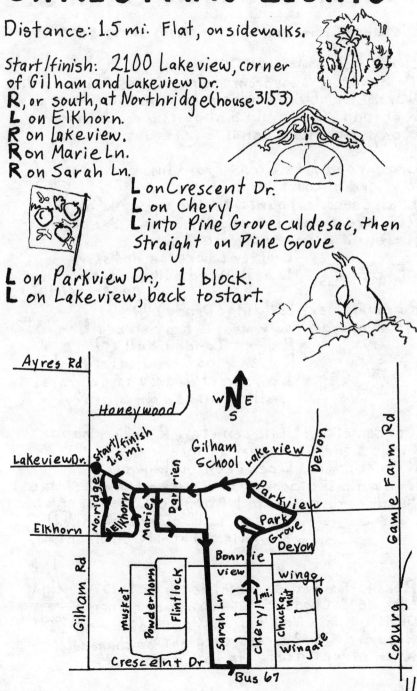

BIG TREES on UO CAMPUS

Distance: 1.5 mi. to 3 mi. ••• show short cuts

Start/finish: Agate and 13th St. parking lot. ①
On Agate, go away from campus. Cross Franklin Blvd.
L on path after bridge over canal. (one block)
R at road. Turn around at posts in road and mural.
R on path before canal. ②

Cross road, **L** to Cross Franklin
R at end of courtyard. ③
L at Cascade fountain. Up steps.
R at street, pass Friendly Hall.
R around Pioneer statue.

$$E_i' = \frac{M_2}{(M_1+M_2)} E_0$$

L after Lawrence Hall sign.
L at Villard Hall. (see history case inside.)

R around next building (Deady). ④
At front, go down walk. **L** at street. **L** on 13th.

Read the book tree sculptures.

R after Condon Hall. ⑤
R at end, jog **L** thru courtyard.
L at street, **L** around to gravel path behind Knight Library.

R at cemetery. **L** into cemetery. **R** on first road.
Circle **L** through cemetery. ⑥
R on road, jog **L** between buildings. ⑦⑧
R on path. **L** diagonal to Pioneer Mother statue.
Return to path. Go left. ⑨ ⑩ Cross street.
At end, **L** to curve **R**. ⑪⑫
L on first path. **R** on street, 13th

† 1910 †

R before kiosk to lot, straight to street. (15th)
L on 15th. Cross 15th and Agate at corner.
On 15th, **R** into Ntrl. Hist. Museum garden.
Return to 15th. Cross, straight to diagonal.
R at street, Agate, to 13th and finish.

Deady Hall

12

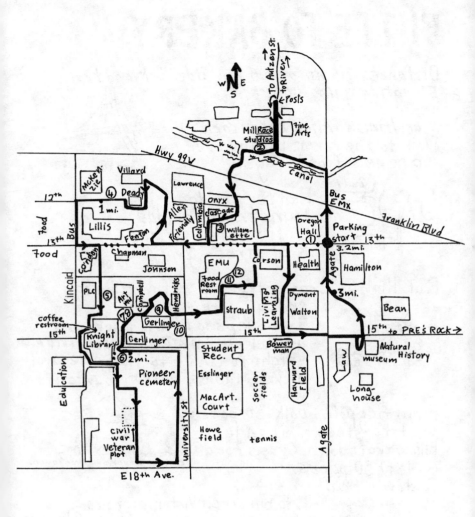

Big Trees on Campus

1. Red Oaks along 13th.
2. Incense Cedar on right.
3. Dawn Redwood in corner.
4. Douglas firs line path.
5. English Oak border park.
6. Two Madrona, broadleaf.
7. California Laurel.
8. European Beech.
9. Black Walnut.
10. Red Maple on right.
11. European White Birch.
12. London plane tree.

BUTTE TO BAKERY

Distance: 2.5 mi. or 3.5 mi. Sidewalk and trail.
Elevation gain: 400 ft.

Start/finish: Alton Baker Park.
Walk to the river. Up and over
   arched foot bridge.

go over this bridge

2nd Ave

Bike path

R after bridge.
L under car bridge.
L off main path, go
R at street, 2nd Ave.

R at High St. Cross street at second ⬦ sign,
            at end of parking lot.
         R up steps to trail. Follow any
         gravel path up. On top, continue
         right to curve to flagpole and
         picnic tables, water fountain.

Relics of a BBQ

From flagpole, walk 30 paces
west to steep trail on left.
Follow trail down. Cross road.
Go left 30 paces.
R down trail.

Spencer Butte beyond downtown.

L to big green Victorian house.
Walk around to view front of house.
Exit on driveway.

Shelton-McMurphy House
on National Historic Register

(For 2.5 mi. go straight to High St.)
(**L** on High. **R** on 2nd Av. to park.)

Shelton-M-Johnson
House Tours #5
T-F 10-1 SS. 1-4
484-0808

R at street (Pearl)
844 Pearl is Palace Bakery.
L on 11th Av. **L** on Hilyard to path.
L on main bike path.
L at fountain, big plaza.
R at street. Cross bridge to park.

Sisters
Peaks in distance

14

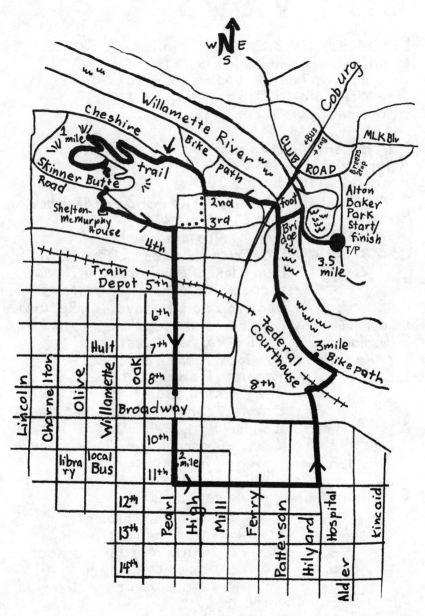

N
W E
S

Willamette River

Coburg

Cheshire

Bike path

MLK Blv

CLUB ROAD

Breeze Shop

1 mile

trail

Skinner Butte Road

Shelton-McMurphy House

2nd

3rd

4th

foot

Bridge

Alton Baker Park Start/finish
T/P

3.5 mile

Train Depot 5th

6th

Federal Courthouse

3 mile Bike path

Hult 7th

8th

8th

Lincoln

Charnelton

Olive

Willamette

Oak

Broadway

10th

library

local Bus

11th

2 mile

12th

13th

14th

Pearl

High

Mill

Ferry

Patterson

Hilyard

Hospital

Alder

Kincaid

Western Trillium
in spring

CITY VIEWS

Distances: 2.3, 3.6, 7.7 or 9.8 miles.
Elevation: 2.3 and 3.6 mi. is 84 ft.
          7.7 mi. is 600 ft.   9.8 mi. is 709 ft.
(For 7.7 mi. start/finish at Monroe & 27th)
(follow directions from ▲ to ▲.

Start/finish: Amazon & 24th
R from parking lot, on 24th
R on McMillan. L up 22nd.
L on Monroe. (for 3.6 mi. R on 26th) R on Van Buren. See ■ below.)
(for 2.3 mi.,   R on 27, one block.
R on Monroe.   (for 7.7 mi. start here) ▲
see * below)   L on Friendly. Cross 28th st. R on 28th
                    L on Adams. R on Tiara. L on Mclean.
→ L at 2010-2070 Mclean, up steps.
                    L at top, do Lindsay Loop. Return.
L at first corner, opposite steps.
R on Blacktail. R at first corner, Lasater.
L on Randy, one block. R on Ridgemont.
L on 29th   R on Blacktail. R on Herald.
                    R on Blacktail, again!
                    L at next corner, Mystic, one block to
                    L on Hawkins, one block.
                    R on Wintercreek. L on Timberline Dr.
At Brighton corner, R down steep, paved path.
Stay on main, downhill path, crossing 4 streets.
R at end (Brittany), where it is flat.
                    At end, cross 18th L one block.
                    R on Quaker. R on bike path.
                    R on foot bridge opposite school.
                    L after bridge onto bark trail.
                    Curve R. L after houses to street, 20th.

Tuliptree leaf.

▲ (for 7.7 mi, R on Monroe to 27th)
* ■ (2.3 and 3.6 mi. R on 20th.)
L on Madison, after path. one block.   R on 19th
R on bike path before So. Eugene HS. to finish.

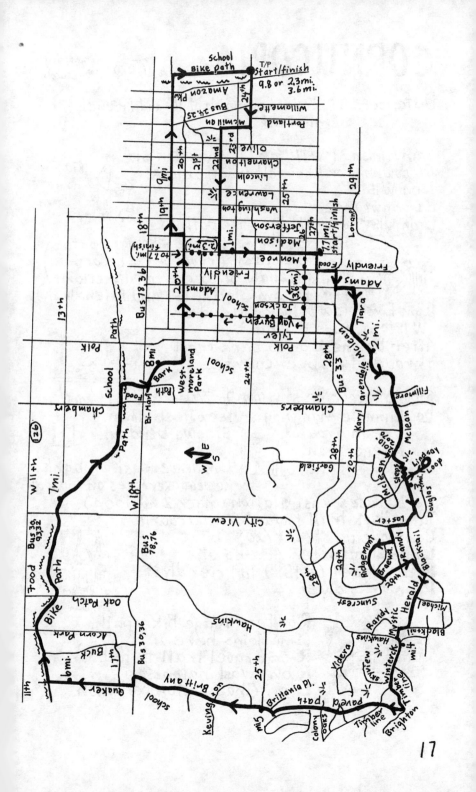

17

CORNUCOPIA

Cornucopia — market, deli 17th ~ Lincoln

Distance: 1 mi., 2 mi. (start/finish at 16th and Friendly).
3.1 mi. Flat

Start/finish at W 17th and Charnelton St.
Go downhill on Charnelton one block.
L on W 16th
R on Lawrence
L on W 15th to Fern Ridge Bike path.

Fern Ridge bike path

(for 1 mi. **L** off the bike path onto
the first gravel path, before
Friendly St. see ✳ for directions.)
(for 2 mi. start at 16th and Friendly St.)

L on first footbridge, Up and over
W 18th St. Pass Bi-Mart.
After bridge, **L** on to bark trail
through frisbee course.

<u>Stop</u> at exercise station. <u>Do</u> 20 pushes off wall.
<u>Do</u> 1 minute hanging.   Keep heels down.
Feet on ground.   Elbows bend out.
Knees bent.

Continue past on bark.
Repeat exercises on 2nd loop.

Go 20 paces past station. (after 2nd loop.)
Take bark trail toward tennis courts.
Continue up street (20th).
L into alley after Adams St.
R at street (W. 18th) to Friendly St.
L on Friendly St.

1661 Washington

1660 Washington

R on Fern Ridge Bike path.
(1 mi. joins here.)
R on gravel trail to 16th.
R on Washington St.
L on Charnelton to finish.

1870 home, barn

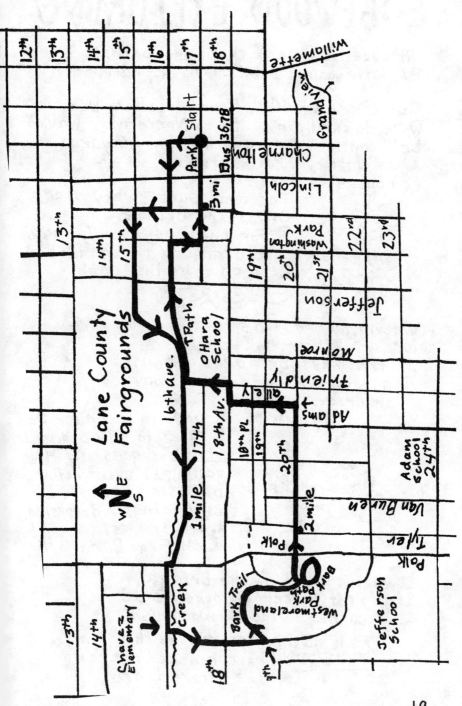

19

EDGEWOOD EXPLORING

Distance: 1 mile with optional paths
Elevation gain: 108 ft. on asphalt path

Start/finish at 40th St. and Brae Burn Dr.
Walk downhill, or south to Normandy Way.
Left on to Normandy Way for 25 yards.
L on Nature Trail between
    houses 4031 and 4047.

The first part is very steep.
Cross the bridge.
R for the easy ¼ mile loop,
    returning to the bridge.
L to go down the path.

When you cross a street,
look right for the path.
At the next bridge; 2 options.
R across the bridge to a 3 way
    intersection.

Here **R** goes to Lockmoor Dr.
L goes to 439 Brookside.
<u>Straight</u> goes up the
valley. It eventually
becomes very steep,
emerging on Brookside.
L on Brookside
L on Brae Burn to 40th

L without crossing the bridge.
L at next street (Brookside Dr.)
L at corner (Brae Burn) to finish.

Private Property
residents & guests
only

When you see this sign, you
have reached the end of
the nature trail.

20

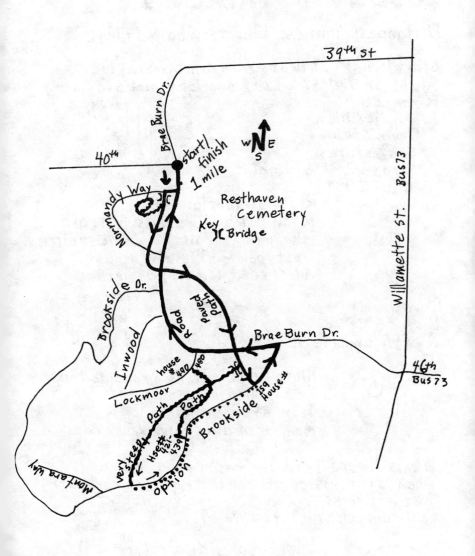

39th st

Brae Burn Dr.

40th

W N E S

start/ finish
1 mile

Normandy Way

Resthaven Cemetery

Key)(Bridge

Brookside Dr.

Inwood

Road

paved path

Brae Burn Dr.

Willamette st. Bus 73

house #400

Lockmoor

Path

)(

H se# 439

Brookside House #

459

46th Bus 73

Montara Way

very steep

option

Path

21

EDGEWOOD TRAILS I

Distance 6.4 miles. Elevation gain 498ft.

Start/finish: 24th St + Amazon parking lot.
Right on 24th St. Left on Portland St.
R on 26th
L on McMillan.
   Down steps
   past stores.
   Cross 29th at light.
   L on 29th

Right on Portland St.
R on 30th. Up steps, to trail.
Take uphill trails to picnic shelter,
(restrooms). Pass the house.
At street (Crest) go left.

R on Olive.
L on 35th
R on Willamette St.

R into cemetery. R on road to top.
Exit right to street, 40th
L on Brae Burn.
R on Normandy Way, 25 yards.

L onto Nature Trail. The first part is steep.
When path crosses street, look right for next path.
Take left forks,
continuing downhill to this sign.

Private Property
residents + guests
only

L on Brookside Dr. (hse #159) at
R on Brae Burn, Cross Willamette to 46th
L on Pearl. R on 41st.
L on Donald. R on 40th
L on 39th. L on path to meadow.
Cross street. Veer left to path
downhill to Tugman Park.
                    (restrooms)

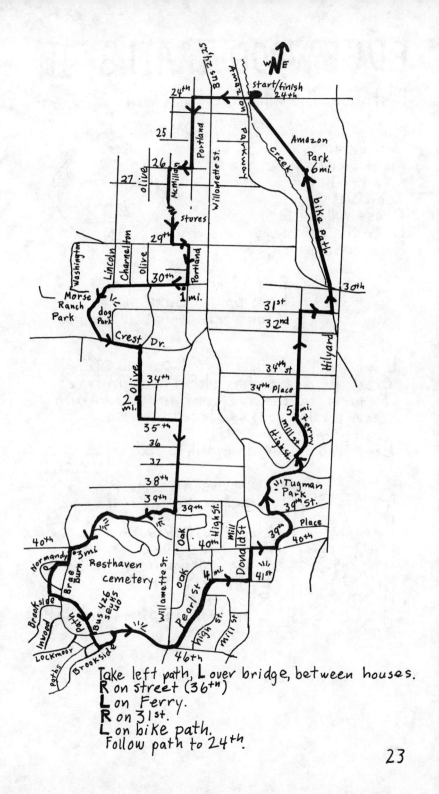

Take left path, L over bridge, between houses.
R on street (36th)
L on Ferry.
R on 31st.
L on bike path.
Follow path to 24th.

EDGEWOOD TRAILS II

Distance 2.4 miles. Elevation gain 222 ft.

Start/finish   40th and Donald St.
West on 40th St.
Right on Oak St.
L. on Pearl St
L. on 39th
Cross Willamette St.
Enter the cemetery.
R on road to top.

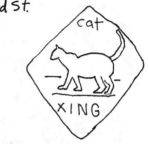

Exit right to street, 40th
L on Brae Burn St.
R on Normandy Way, about 25 yards

L onto Nature Trail. The first part is STEEP!
Cross bridge. R for short loop in trees.
Return to bridge, continue downhill.
When path crosses street,
look right for trail.
Left forks go downhill, to end.

Private Property
residents & guests
only

When you see this sign,
you reached the end of the trail.

L on Brookside Dr. to corner.
R on Brae Burn
Cross Willamette St. to 46th
L on Pearl St.
R on 41st.
L on Donald St. to 40th to finish.

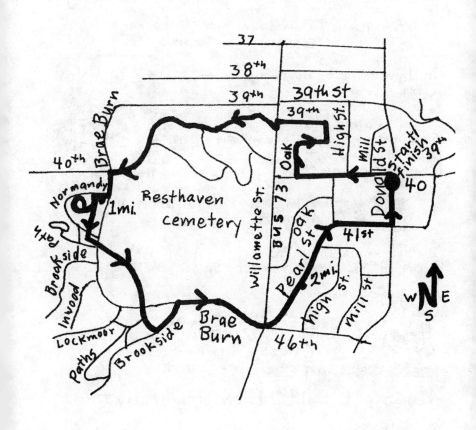

37

38th

39th

39th St

39th

39th

High St.

Oak

Brae Burn

40th

Normandy

1 mi.

Resthaven cemetery

Willamette St.

Bus 73

Mill

Start finish

Donald St

40

Pearl St.

Oak

41st

2 mi.

high st.

Mill st

Brookside

Inwood

Lockmoor

Paths

Brookside

Brae Burn

46th

W N E S

Fall crocus

25

ELK STREET

Distance: 1.5 mi, 2.5 mi., or 3.1 mi. 135 ft. elevation gain.

Start/finish: 24th and University St. by park.
seasonal restrooms.

On University, go north, uphill to 23rd.
R on 23rd. St.
L on Columbia, crossing
old trolley tracks.
Straight and up to 22nd on right.
L on Fairmount.
R on McMorran St. at

2315 memoran
home of
U.O. President

At corner, **L** to Fairmount.
R on Fairmount.

(for 1.5 mi. **L** on Moss.
L on 19th. **L** on University St.)

gable
top

R on Elk St. **L** at corner.
Pass # 2017 to path and steps.
Cross Summit Street.
R on Fairmount.

Path connects
Elk St. to Summit St.

(for 2.5 mi, **L** on 19th. **L** on University St.)

L on 15th.
L on Villard St.
R on 19th.
L on University St.

1910 E.15th
Maude Kerns

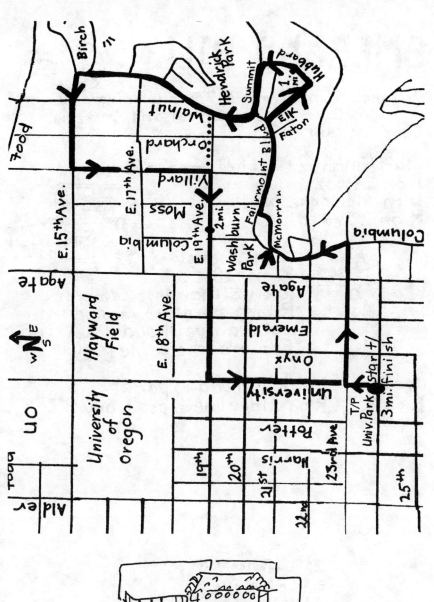

1262 E. 19th Ave.

EMERALD HILL

mason symbol on tombstone

Distance: 1.5 mi. from 24th St. and University.
            2.5 mi. from 24th St. and Amazon.
Elevation gain: 116 ft.

Start/finish: 24th St. and Amazon Parkway.
L on 24th St.
L on Alder one block.
R on 23rd St.

mausoleum   Hope Abbey
Egyptian Revival Style

wild tall OREGON Grape

R on Emerald
R on 28th.
R on Elinor, into cemetery
R fork in path to mausoleum.
Take gravel road down to exit.
Explore the cemetery.

(for 1.5 mi. straight at road to park.)
L on 25th. **R** on Alder one block. **L** on 24th.

25th and Potter St. NW corner
Exact miniature
of Stonehenge in England,
lines up with equinox.

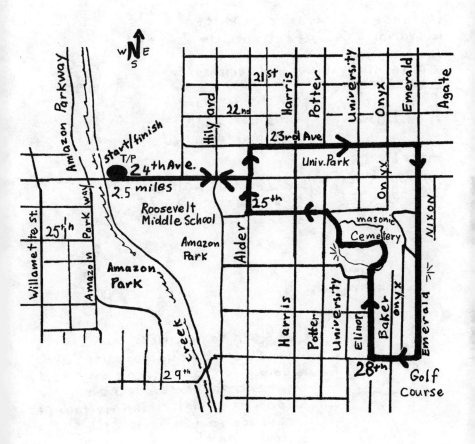

FAIRMOUNT TRAIL

Distance: 2, 2.5 or 4 miles
Elevation: 227 ft gain or 2 mi. flat

Start/finish at 24th and University.
L on 24th Ave.
L on Alder.
R on 23nd.　　(for 2.5 mi. start/
　　　　　　　　finish at 24th
　　　　　　　　and University.)

University Park
Playground

(for 2mi. flat walk; at 23+Agate,
L on Agate, **L** on 21st
L on Alder, **R** on 24th to end)

L on Columbia
R on Fairmount Blvd.

trail

fairmount

21+Agate

L at fork to Hendricks Park.
Where curbs end, opposite #2800,
L down to trail (or stay on road.)
Where trail comes to road,
L on path, past drinking fountain
Cross road (Summit St.)
L down path.

L
R on to Fairmount Blvd.
L on 21st
R on Alder
　on 24th to finish.

Path

view south
Spencer Butte

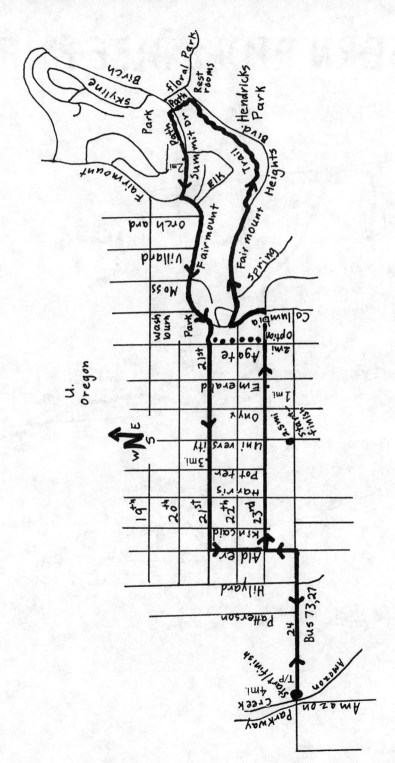

31

FERN RIDGE BIKE PATH

● some easy access points

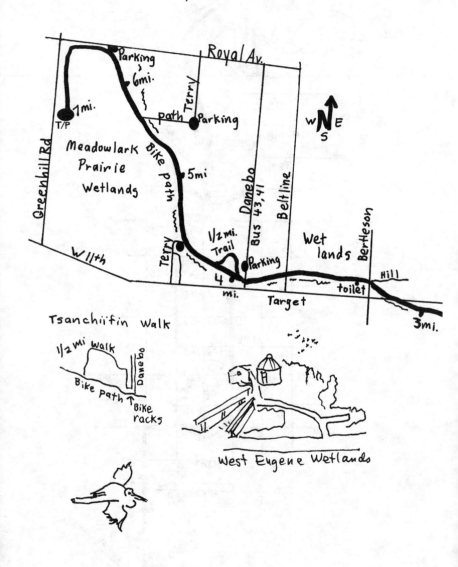

Tsanchiifin Walk

West Eugene Wetlands

FERN RIDGE BIKE PATH

Distance: 7 miles from 15th and Jefferson to end at parking lot on Greenhill Rd.

Access streets for shorter options:
- Polk St. • Oak Patch • Acorn Park st.
- Bertleson and Hill • Danebo: Wetland office lot.
- Terry off W. 11th and Royal Av.
- Royal Ave • Greenhill Rd.

Flat, paved bike path along Amazon Creek.

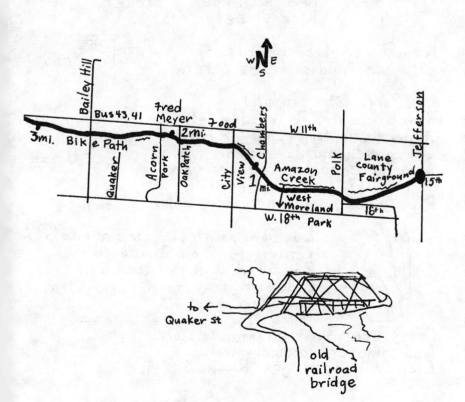

to ←
Quaker St

old
railroad
bridge

FOUR CREEKS

Distance: 2 mi. flat OR 2.5 mi, 3.5 mi, 7 mi. hilly
Elevation gain: 270 ft   or 540 ft on 7 mi. option

Start/finish: 24th and Amazon parking lot.
R on 24th. L on Portland.
R on 26th. L on McMillan.
Down steps. Past stores.
Cross 29th at light. (2 mi. option is
L on 29th   (L on 29th to
R on Portland.   (bike path. L on path to finish.)
(See map for 2.5 mi. and 3.5 mi. options.)

Wayne Morse Ranch Park

R on 30th, up steps, up trail.
Take uphill trails to picnic
    shelter at top of hill, restrooms.
Pass the house, to street.
R on street (Crest).

R on Storey. L on Lorane.
Stay on right side. Be careful.

L on Paige (steep uphill)
R on Bryceler. R on Edendale.
At dead end, look right for trail.
Cross meadow. L on trail
around school. Exit school yard
to the left. Up to road (crest.)
R on Crest, which becomes Blanton.

to trail

L on Sandpointe. Do loop at end, (OR NOT!)
return to R on Sundance.
R on Sundial, R past guardrail.
L down to trail. follow through trees.
Emerge on 40th

Cross Brae Burn. Go into cemetery.
L on cemetery road, downhill.
L on Willamette, jog R on 39th Ave.

34

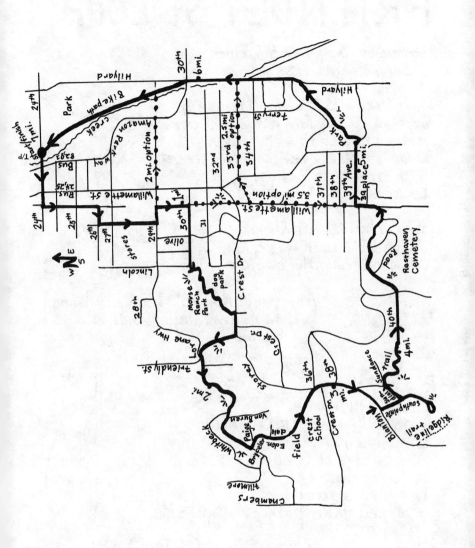

Cross Donald St.,
L on path to Tugman Park. (rest rooms)
L at street (Hilyard).
Cross 30th
L onto path, back to finish.

FRIENDLY St. LOOP

Distance: 3.5, 4 or 5.5 miles
Elevation gain: 434 ft.

Start/finish 15th and Jefferson st.
West on 15th to Fern Ridge bike path.
After crossing Polk St. turn
L on bridge over creek + street.
R in front of school
L at street (Fillmore)

(for 3.5 mile, **L** at Almaden
  L on 28th **L** on Tyler, **R** on 27th
  L on Friendly back to 15th)

garden
art

(for 4 mile, **R** on 28th **L** on Chambers.
  L on Arendale, follow directions
    below *)

old
saw

gate
1795
W. 28th

R on 28th
L on City View
R on 29th, curves to Kendrick.
L on Karyl st.
Cross Street (Chambers) Careful!
R to corner.
L on Arendale *
  at end, take path on right side.

2778
Friendly

J·TEA

Cross Street (Mclean). go Left.
R on Ingalls, straight on Tiara.
L at 917, 997 around cul de sac.
  Continue down Tiara.

Blue Bus - 2584 Friendly St.

L on Adams st.
R on 28th
L on Friendly St.
R on bike path to start/finish.

36

Here rests a Wood man of the World 1852-1905

GILLESPIE BUTTE

Distance: 1 mi. Start/finish at Debrick + Clinton St.
  3 mi. Start/finish at Valley River Inn.
  6 mi. Start/finish at Alton Baker Park.
Elevation: 114 ft. gain up Crenshaw St.

Start/finish: Alton Baker Park.
Walk to river.
R on bike path.
At the end of Valley River Inn's
  deck, go **R**ight up steps.
Straight onto Valley River Way. (for 3 mi.
Stay on right-hand side.   (Start here.)

Eugene Legacy Tree
atop Gillespie Butte

1218
Crenshaw bench   turtle

R at light. Up and over Delta Hwy.
L on Willagillespie.
R on Clinton. (for 1 mi.
L on Debrick. (start here.)
R on Crenshaw.

In cemetery, take right path
up to crest of hill. Explore the
cemetery at the far end.
Exit on road to right, onto Crenshaw.

Young

L at Debrick **R** on Clinton
L on Willagillespie. (for 3 mi, return)
             (over Delta Hwy)

L on Country Club Road.
R at first corner.
L at street (Willagillespie).

Spencer Butte
behind Skinner Butte

R at traffic light.
Under bridge. Straight to path
back to park.

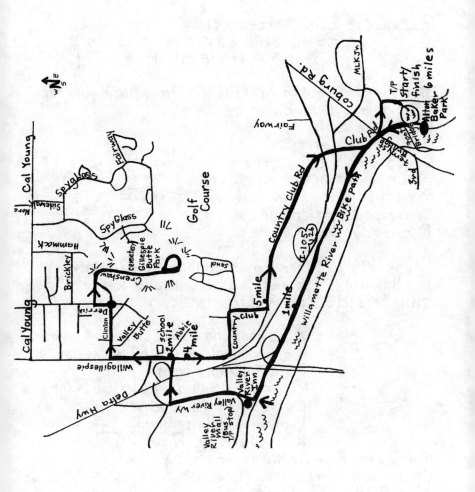

Here rests
a Wood man
of the World.
1852-1905

HAWKIN'S HAUNTS

Distance: 2 mi. 30 ft. elevation
3.6 mi. 61 ft. elevation
5.3 mi. 347 ft. elevation

Start/finish at Acorn Park, at W15th and Buck park lot.
Walk downhill on Buck St.
R on bike path.
Under first street.
Cross Oak Patch st., then
after apartments on right,
R on trail through meadow.
L around apartments.
R onto Wilson Court.

Cross W18th St. (for 2mi: **R** on 18th. **R** on Quaker.
Up Hawkins   **R** on 17th **L** on Brittany **R** on 16th.
on left side. **L** on Buck to Acorn Park.

1700 Wilson Court
garden art

R across Hawkins onto So. Lambert.
R after ½ block into Mulkey Cemetery.
Find Hawkins family plot.
Return to So. Lambert. Go **R**ight.
Curve left to Greiner.
L on Park Hill one block.
R on Stansby. **R** on 25th.

(for 3.6 mi. **R** on Brittany to 18th.)
(Then follow directions from ✱)
L on Brittany ½ block.
At Bus 36 sign, **L**eft on path.
When you cross the 4th street,
look right for path by 2893.
Path ends at Brighton and Timberline.

L on Timberline.
R on Wilshire. **L** at 3727-3779 sign.
Straight to path between 3575 - 3745.
R at street (Blackburn).

R on Kevington.
L on Brittany.(✳ 3.6 mi. joins here.)
Cross W18ᵗʰ. **L** ½ block.
R on Quaker St. **R** on W17ᵗʰ
L on Brittany. **R** on W16ᵗʰ.
L on Buck to Acorn Park.

Hawkin's Barn at 19ᵗʰ & Hawkins

41

HISTORIC HOMES

Distance: 2 mi., 3.2 mi. or 4.7 mi. Flat.

Start/finish: Alton Baker Park.

Walk to the river. Go over the arched foot bridge.
L after bridge.
L through EWEB plaza.
R on bike path.

faded sign on side reads
W.H. ABRAHAMS' CIDER FACTORY and FRUIT DRYER

R at to Hilyard sign. Cross r.r. tracks.
L at 602 driveway to see old cider mill. 1883.
(for 2 mi., return to park.)
Return to Hilyard st.
Cross Hilyard. Go Right.

Gamma Phi Beta sorority

R on 11th st, one block.
L on Patterson, one block.
R on 12th

mural

12th and High St.

(for 3.2 mi.
R on Willamette St.
R on 5th see ✱ below.)

170 E. 12th Oldest house in Eugene.

L on Washington. Cross 13th. Go Right.
Lane Co. History Museum. 740 W. 13th
open 10-4. Tues. through Sat. $2.

Spencer Butte

R on Monroe.
R on 5th ✱
L on High. **L** on 3rd. **R** on Pearl.
R on 2nd.

L to path under bridge.
R to go up, over foot bridge.

First Christian Church
12th and Oak St.

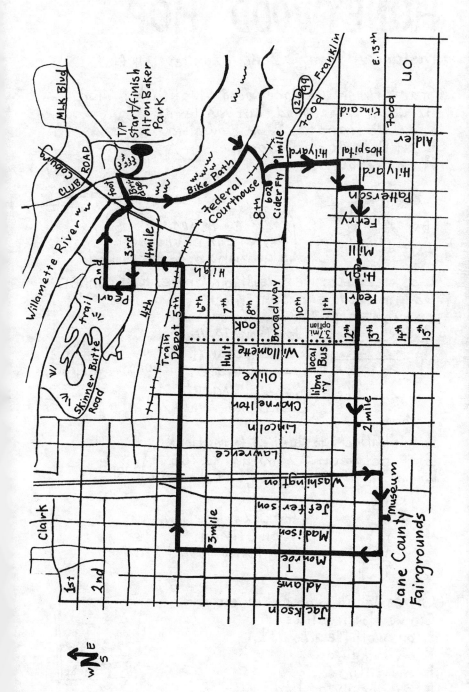

43

HONEYWOOD HOP

Distance: 2 mi., 3.2 mi, 4.2 miles. All flat.

Start/finish: On Honeywood St. at Gilham Rd.
Go down Honeywood, curves left.
R on Wester St. **R** on Downing.
L on Dale. **R** on Devon Av.
R on Lakeview.

(for 2 mi. option,
Stay on Lakeview.
R on Gilham to Honeywood.

L at next corner, 2308 Park Grove. **R** at corner.
Go into cul de sac, continue
on right, past 2318 Park Grove

L on Bonnie View.
R on Chuckanut.
L on Wingate.
R on Chuckanut.
L on Bonnie View.
} a loop

(1910 chuckanut)

R on Flintlock, to Musket, to Flintlock.
Exit between #2985 and #2963.
L on Sarah. **L** at end, on Lakeview.
} a loop

(for 3.2 mi. option.
R on Gilham
R on Honeywood to finish.

Cross Gilham on Lakeview Dr.
Curve to Metolius.
L on Wolf Meadows Ln.
R on Lakeview
L on Gilham.
R on Honeywood to finish.

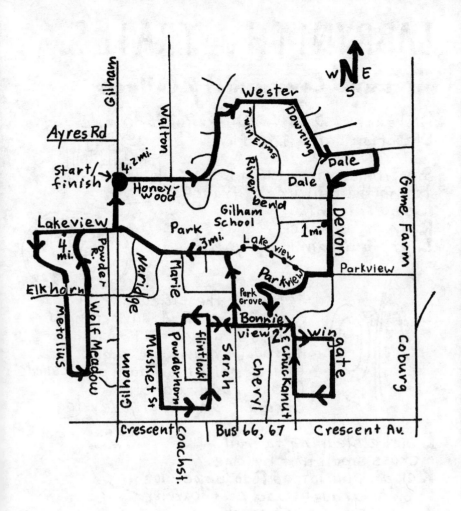

Ayres Rd

Gilham

Walton

Wester

Downing

Twin Elms

Dale

N
W E
S

Start/
finish

4.2 mi.

Honey-
wood

Riverbend

Dale

Game Farm

Gilham
School

1 mi

Devon

Lakeview

Park

.3 mi.

Lakeview

Parkview

Parkview

Coburg

4 mi.

Powder Pt.

Maridge

Marie

Park Grove

Elkhorn

Metolius

Wolf Meadow

Gilham

Musket St

Powderhorn

Flintlock

Sarah

Bonnie view

Cheryl

E Chuckanut

.2

Wingate

Crescent

Coach St.

Bus 66, 67

Crescent Av.

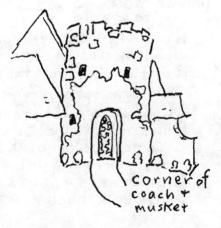

corner of
coach + musket

45

LABRYNITH and TRAILS

at Lane Community College

Distance: .5 mile, or 1.25, 2.25 or 3 mile
Elevation gain: 130 ft.

Start/finish at building **1**
facing the building entrance,
L on sidewalk
R in to garden
L at fountain to labrynith.

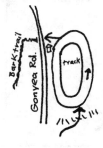

Return to the sidewalk.
R on side walk. Around tennis
courts, **L** down to track.
Half way around the track,
exit straight on path past 2 sheds.
Cross road - careful!
Straight onto trail, over log.

L in the clearing, to trail,
cross small foot bridge.

view from
the receiver.

R at parking lot, go **R** to upper lot.
R on to gravel road, past barrier,
L on the gravel road.
(for 1.25 mi, return to start.)

R at first yellow barrier.
Uphill on gravel road to receiver.
R of the receiver, take trail down.
(for 2.5 mi. option, straight on road,
L on bark trail. **L** by tennis, to start.)
R on Eastway Dr. **L** on to trail.
L on road. **R** on bark trail at
first parking lot. Stay on trail,
L at tennis courts onto
sidewalk back to start.

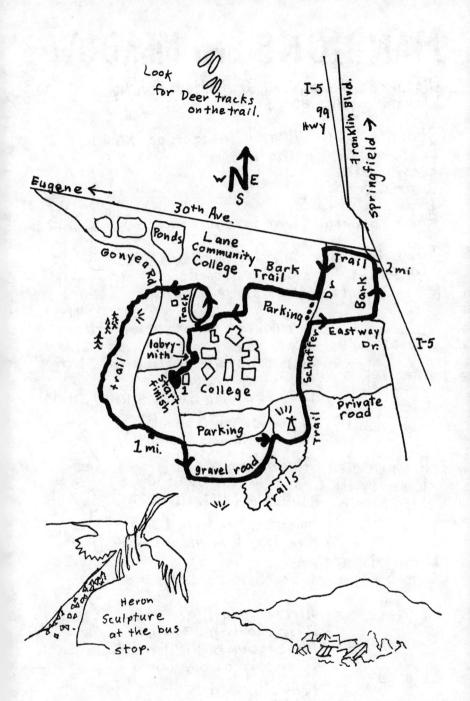

Look for Deer tracks on the trail.

Heron Sculpture at the bus stop.

MANSIONS and MEADOW

Distance: 4.4 mi, 7 mi, or 9 miles, all hilly
Elevation gain: 834 ft.

Start/finish: 24th and Amazon parking lot.
Left on 24th, going east.
L on Alder
R on 23rd.
L on Columbia.
R on Fairmount. L at fork in road.

Just before next intersection, (Floral Hill Rd.)
look RIGHT for stone restrooms.
R on the trail past stone building.

2855 Capitol
colorful lampposts

Straight at large stone marker.
L at the fork in the trail.
You emerge on Capitol Blvd,
curves around.
L at Spring Blvd, sharp turn.
　(4.4 mi. option. R on 27th)
　(R on Columbia. L on 24th)

R on Central. At mailbox 2891,
L on trail. Cross bridge over 30th.
Up Spring Blvd. R on Firland St.
　(7 mi. option. R on Agate. L on 31st)
　(R on 32nd. R on Alder. L on 24th)

L on Agate.
L to Spring, at So. Shasta Loop sign.

At trail sign, go
R on downhill trail.
Emerge on old Dillard. L on Snell.
R on Amazon Dr.

R on Kincaid St.
At 35th L on to Alder.
L on 24th, back to finish.

48

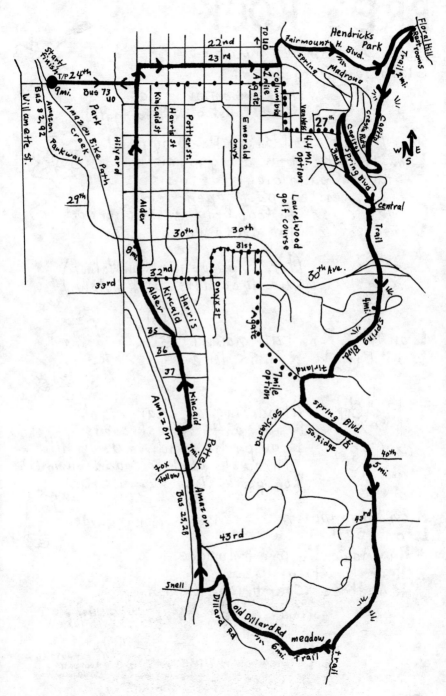

49

PRE's ROCK

Distance: 2.5mi, 4.5mi. or 6.5mi
Elevation gain: 300 ft.

(for 2.5mi.option - flat
start/finish at 15th and Agate.)

Start/finish Alton Baker Park by pond.
L on to bike path along river.
  Stay on path along river
  for 2miles, past open field.
R over river on foot bridge. (Knickerbocker)
L at traffic light on to Walnut.

(for 4.5mi. option, R on Walnut.)
(Use directions at * below.)

L on 15th **R** on Fairmount
L on Birch. **R** on Skyline

At parking lot, bear right.
R on path to restrooms.
R on paths winding down hill.
  through park to road (Summit).
R on path along Summit Dr.

Hendricks Park

R on Fairmount.   1568 Fairmount garden
L on 15th
***R** on Agate. **L** before footbridge.
 L at fountain-plaza.
 R at street. Over bridge to finish.

Skinner Butte — downtown — view on skyline Dr. — Gillespie Butte — Autzen football stadium — Willamette River

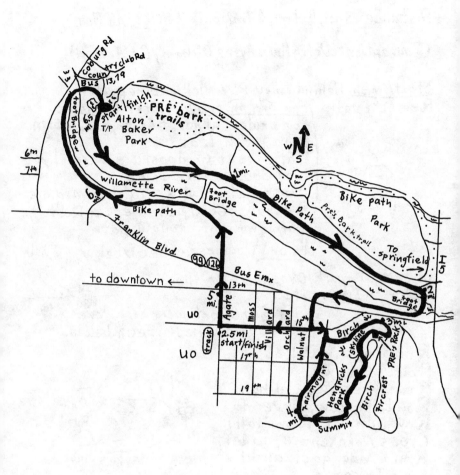

Coburg Rd
country club Rd
Bus 13, 79
foot Bridge
6.5 mi.
start/finish
Alton
T/P Baker
Park
PRE'bark trails

6th
7th

Willamette River
foot Bridge
Bike path
6m.
Franklin Blvd
99 026

1 mi.
Bike Path
Bike path
Park
PRE'bark trail
TO springfield
I 5

to downtown ←
Bus Emx
13th
5 mi.
UO
Agate
moss
Villard
orchard
15th
Birch
foot Bridge
2mi.

UO
track
2.5mi
start/finish
17th
Walnut
Fairmount (Skyline)
Hendricks Park
Birch
Fircrest
PRE's Rock
3mi.

19th
4 mi.
Summit
Birch

W N E S

51

PRETTY PONDS

Distance: 3 mi, 5.4 mi, 6.1 mi, or 8.7 miles. All flat.

(3 mi. option: Delta Hwy. Ayres, Gilham, Gr. Acres.)

<u>Start/finish:</u> Behind Valley River Mall on bike path.
R on bike path.

1520 Montrey
flat farmer

For 5.4 mi. option, after Owosso footbridge at Adopt-A-Path, M. Booth sign.
R on path, **L** at fork.
L at street: Goodpasture Lakes Lp.
L at Goodpasture Is. Rd.
Cross Delta Hwy at light. Immediate **R** across Goodpasture Is. Rd. to path on Right. follow path.
R on Willagillespie. See ◆ below

At end of path, Cross Delta Hwy.
L for <u>8.7 mi.</u> route.

(for <u>6.1 mi</u>, Continue on Gr. Acres.)
(**R** on Norakenzie. See ✳ below.)

1580 Montrey

R on Stapp. **L** Delta Pines.
R on Delta Hwy.
R on Ayres. **R** on Gilham.
R on Lakeview, curves to
R on Gilham. **R** on Holly.
Cross Norakenzie, go left.
R on Linda, go straight. ✳
L on Tabor.

Ayres view

L on Larkspur. **R** on Montrey. **R** on Norakenzie.
R on Bond. **L** on Fir Acres.
Cross Cal Young.
Straight to Debrick.

1350 Fir Acres

R on Clinton.
L on Willagillespie.
At light, cross Abbie. ◆
R on Valley River Dr. over highway.
L at light. **R** past Valley River Inn.
Down steps. **R** on path to finish.

1256 Fir Acres

52

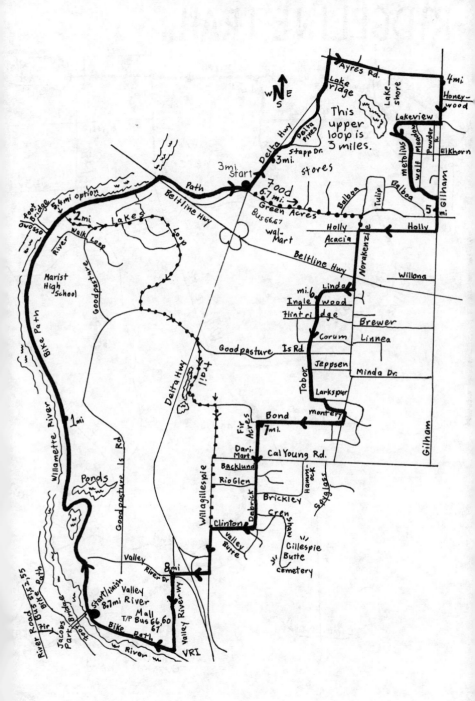

53

RIDGELINE TRAIL

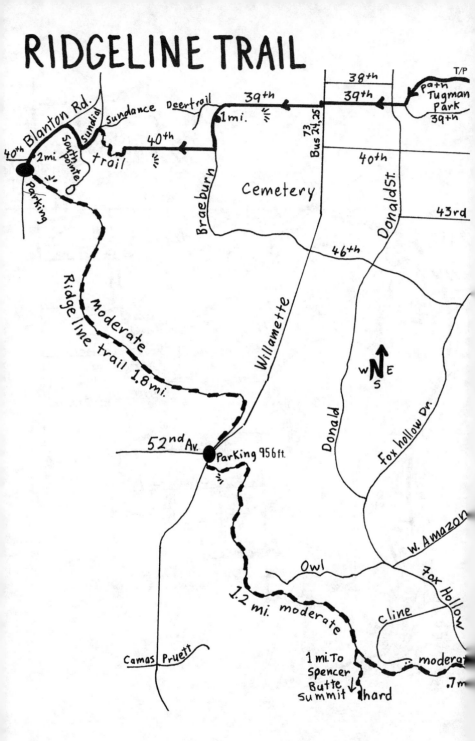

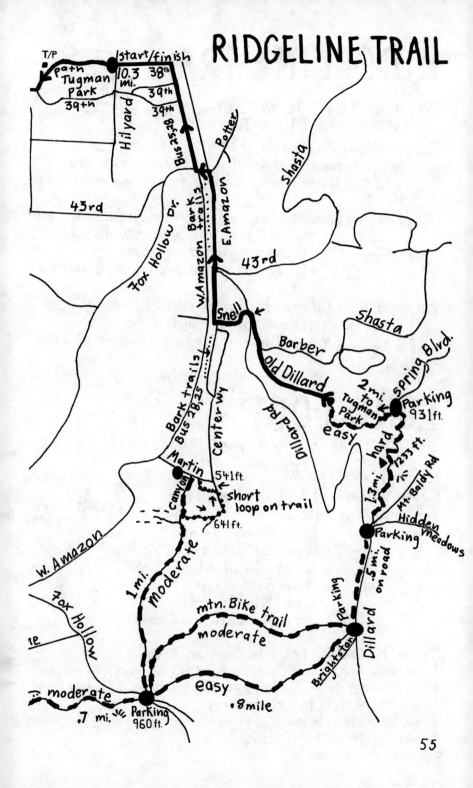

RIDGELINE TRAIL

T/P
path
Tugman Park
39th

start/finish
10.3 mi. 38th
39th
39th

Hilyard

Bus 25,28

W. Amazon Bark trails

Potter

E. Amazon

43rd

Fox Hollow Dr.

Snell

Barber

Shasta

Shasta

Old Dillard

2 mi. to Tugman Park
easy

Spring Blvd.

Parking 931 ft.

hard

1233 ft.
1.3 mi.

Mt. Baldy Rd.

Bark trails
Bus 28,25

Center wy

Dillard Rd

Martin

541 ft.

short loop on trail

641 ft.

Canyon

Hidden Meadows

Parking

.5 mi. on road

Dillard

1 mi.
moderate

W. Amazon

Fox Hollow

1e

mtn. bike trail
moderate

Parking

Brightston

easy

.8 mile

moderate

.7 mi.

Parking 960 ft.

55

RIDGELINE TRAIL

Distance: 1.6 mi. to 10.3 mi. loop, Many options.
   STAY on the Main Trail.

Easy   •From Fox Hollow parking lot, walk
      toward Dillard and back. Take the
      upper, right hand trail. See below at *.

Moderate •From Martin, up Canyon Dr. and back: 2mi.
      •From 52nd + Willamette: walk the
       trail either direction.
      •From Fox Hollow toward Willamette st.

Hard •From Dillard to Spring Blvd. 1.3 mi.
      •Up Spencer Butte Summit.
      •Long loop: Tugman Park start/finish. 10.3 mi.

LONG LOOP 10.3 mi.
Hilly!

Start/finish at 38th and Hilyard. (Restrooms.)
L past playground, uphill path.
R at street! (39th)
Cross Willamette St, jog **L** then **R** to
continue up 39th.

   L on Brae Burn.
   R on 40th. Take trail.
   L onto Sundial.
   R on So. Pointe
   L on Blanton to
      trail head. (2 mi. mark)

*from
Fox Hollow
Parking.

up ↑ to
Willam-
ette St.

Bikes>

easy

down to
Canyon Dr.

to
Dillard

Douglas
fir cone

Follow Ridgeline trail to Spring Blvd.
L down trail at Spring Blvd. (2 mi. back to finish.)
L on Snell. **R** on E. Amazon Wy: Bark trail along creek.
L on Fox Hollow to cross creek.
R on W. Amazon Wy.
L on 38th st. to finish.

RIDGELINE SHORT LOOP

Distance: .5 mile   Elevation gain: 101 feet.

Start/finish: Martin Dr. and Canyon Dr.
Go up Canyon Dr. to trail.
L when cross a trail, in 500 ft.
L at next fork in trail.
Emerge on street (Center Way).
L at first corner (Overbrook).
Curve left through houses.
L at corner (Martin) to finish.

at
Cold Spring Way
and Martin

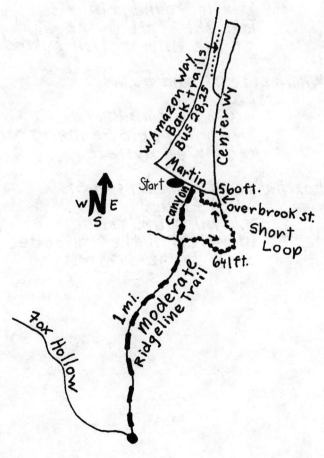

RIDGELINE to SUMMIT

caution: There are several faint trails
         near the top. Going up, pick any
         up hill path. You may just pick
         your way through and over the
         rocks.
         Coming down, it is EASY to become
         confused about the right trail.
         Use a compass to help you.

• From Spencer Butte Park on Willamette St.
         791 ft. up
         1 mile round trip.
         Take the trail to the right
         of the information board.

• From Willamette St. and 52nd.
         1,109 ft. up.
         4.4 mile round trip
         Turn right onto Summit trail.
         It is well posted.

• From Fox Hollow at Christensen St.
         1,105 ft. up.
         3.4 mi. round trip.
         Turn left at the well-posted
         sign to the summit.

SPENCER BUTTE SUMMIT

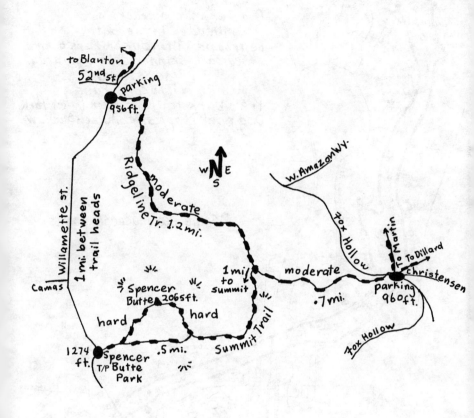

to Blanton
52nd st.
parking
956 ft.

Ridgeline Tr. 1.2 mi.
moderate

Willamette st.
1 mi. between trail heads

Camas

W N E S

W. Amazon Wy.
Fox Hollow

to Marin
to Dillard
christensen

1 mi to summit
moderate
.7 mi.
parking
960 ft.

Spencer Butte 2065 ft.
Summit Trail

hard   hard

Fox Hollow

1274 ft.
Spencer
T/P Butte
Park
.5 mi.

59

RIVER BIKE PATH

Paved path along river. Flat.
See map for distance between six
    foot bridges.
Quarter mile markers are
    embedded in the path.
Restrooms: Alton Baker Park always.
    Seasonal: Skinner Butte play area.
        Rose Garden
            M. Jacobs Park
Pre's bark trails in Alton Baker Park.
Dog park is opposite Autzen Stadium.

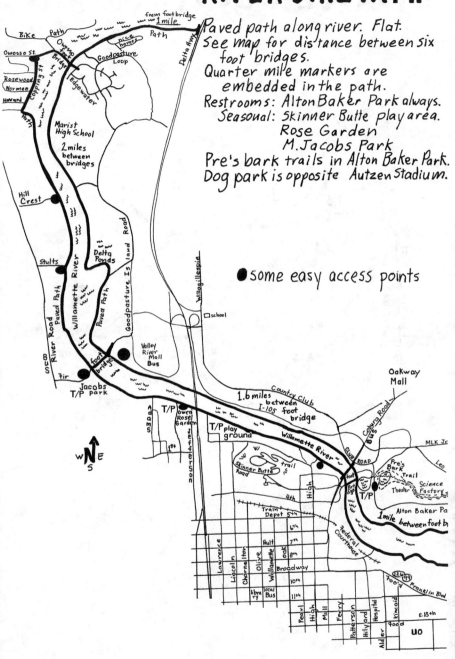

● some easy access points

BIKE PATH ETIQUETTE

Walk or ride on right side.
Keep 2 abreast to let people pass.
Announce your presence when
    passing. "On your left."
Dogs must be leashed. It's the law.
Scoop dog poop.
Use a light when dark.
Nod, smile, say hello to everyone.

Bus: Valley River Mall. Bike path
    is behind mall, along river.

The Sun

Spencer Butte

Bike path along Willamette River

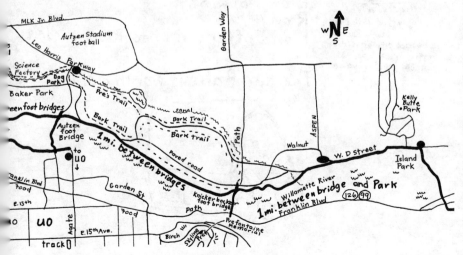

ROSE GARDEN ROUTE

Distance: 4 mi. or 6 mi. Flat.

Start/finish: Rose Garden on north end of Jefferson St. Seasonal restrooms. From parking lot, walk through Rose Garden to bike path.
R on bike path 1¼ mi.
After big plaza of EWEB,
R at this sign

[to → Hilyard]

Cross railroad tracks.
L onto street (Hilyard).
R on 11ᵗʰ Av. for one block.
Cross Patterson.
L on Patterson.
R on 15ᵗʰ Av.

fine homes along canal.

1516 Mill st.
Lovely Blues
· beveled shiplap siding
· river rock edging
· great weathervane

(For 4 mi. **R** on Lincoln
L on bike path to Rose Garden.)

Where 15ᵗʰ ends, continue on Fern Ridge Bike Path.
R on Polk st.
R on 4ᵗʰ Av.
L on Jefferson st. to Rose Garden.

The Red Barn is worth a stop.

RED BARN

Natural foods 4th and Blair

owl and otter sculpture. 1022 4th

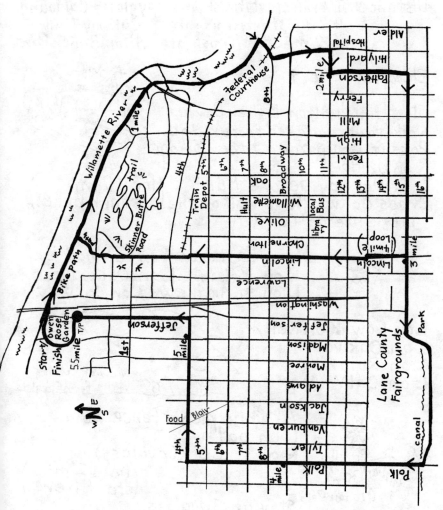

EWEB fountain

turret at 588 W. 11th

SPYGLASS

Distance: 1.2 mi. start/finish at   Spyglass + Cal Young
         4.2 mi. start/finish at   Oakway Mall.
         6.2 mi. start/finish at   Alton Baker Park

Elevation: 92 ft.

Start/finish Alton Baker Park.
Walk toward arched footbridge.
Pass it. Go up ramp to car bridge.
R on bridge.
L at Oakway, before Mall.   (for 4.2 mi.
Cross Oakway. **R** to walk on the   start here.)
   left side of Oakway.

Historic
Cal Young
Ox Yoke Farm 1852

L on Eastway. **R** on Fairway Lp.
R on Kristin. **L** on Oakway,
L on St. Andrews **L** on Oakway.

L on Law. **R** on Keith.
L on Oakway
L on Roland.
L on Cal Young.

View of Coburg
hills from Spyglass

Palm
tree
at
(720 fair Oaks

At white picket fence, go
L on path.
R at street (Spyglass)
              (for 1.2 mi.
              (start here.)

Stay on Spyglass.
It circles around and you
     arrive back here.
Return to Cal Young on the path.
R on Cal Young.
R on Oakway. Stay on Oakway
back to the park, the way you came.

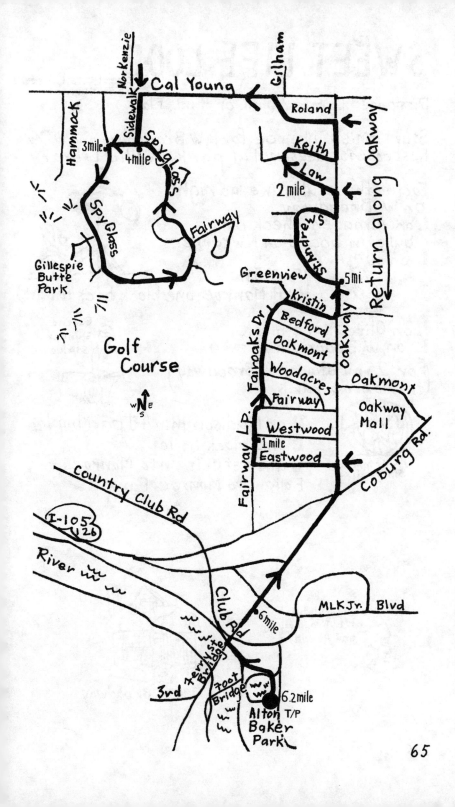

SWEET LIFE LOOP

Distance: 1.5 mi., 2.5 mi., or 4 mi. Flat.

Start/finish: Monroe Park, W. Broadway and 10th Av.
Restrooms: seasonal at park. Public Library.

Facing this sculpture, go right
on W. Broadway.
L on Almaden. check out
  bulletin board on NW corner.
L on 10th Av.

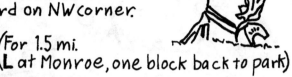

(For 1.5 mi.
L at Monroe, one block back to park)

L on Olive St. one block.
L on W. Broadway.
(For 2.5 mi. stay on W. Broadway)
(to Monroe Park.

Eugene
Skinner
Statue

Millstone
315 Madison

R on Madison into 4-J parking lot.
L one block in lot.
L at first exit onto Monroe.
Follow to Monroe Park.

stone sculpture
at. W. Broadway
and Almaden.

790 W. Broadway

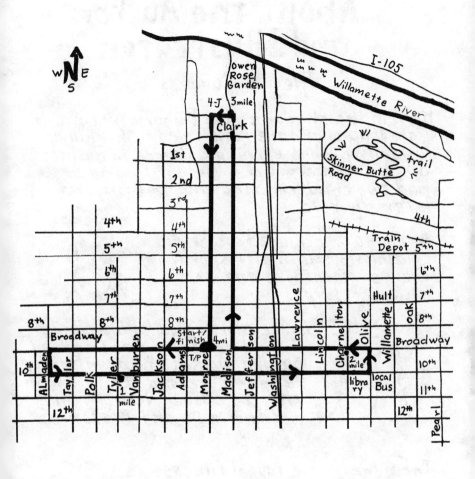

Map labels:

W N E S

I-105

Willamette River

Owen Rose Garden

4-J .3mile

Clark

1st
2nd
3rd
4th   4th
5th   5th
6th   6th
7th   7th
8th   8th

Skinner Butte Road

trail

Train Depot 5th

4th

6th

7th   Hult
8th   Oak

Broadway   Broadway

Almaden
Taylor
Polk
Tyler
Vanburen
Jackson
Adams
Monroe
Madison
Jefferson
Washington
Lawrence
Lincoln
Charnelton
Olive
Willamette

Start/finish   4mi
T/P

.1 mile

.2 mile

library   local Bus

10th
11th
12th   12th

Pearl

· 1006 Taylor Chambers House.
· Painted Lady
· Queen Anne style.
· 3 types of shingles.
· 7 colors.

Dragon tails

sun burst

About the Author and Illustrator

Tyler E. Burgess

Born in the shadow of the Bighorn mountains, I grew up on a cattle ranch near Sheridan, Wyoming. While earning a degree in Business at the University of Wyoming, I married, had two children, Sara and Damon, and later divorced.

In my 40's, I played soccer, did triathlons, solo multi-sport events, marathons and solo back pack trips.

Since starting Walk With Me in 2000 I have organized and led guided walking trips in France, England, Ireland, Italy and Morocco. Also in New York City, Washington DC and Boston.

In Eugene I have taught fitness walking classes at the University of Oregon, Lane Community College and coached marathon walking training.

The four Walk With Me marathons donated thousands of dollars to local charities.

other books: Walking Made Powerful
How to Walk a Marathon, 26.2 Tips
Tyler's Travel Sketchbook Diary